I0814246

Diplodocus

by Julie Murray

Dash!
LEVELED READERS
An Imprint of Abdo Zoom • abdobooks.com

Level 1 – Beginning
Short and simple sentences with familiar words or patterns for children who are beginning to understand how letters and sounds go together.

Level 2 – Emerging
Longer words and sentences with more complex language patterns for readers who are practicing common words and letter sounds.

Level 3 – Transitional
More developed language and vocabulary for readers who are becoming more independent.

abdobooks.com

Published by Abdo Zoom, a division of ABDO, PO Box 398166, Minneapolis, Minnesota 55439.

Printed in the United States of America, North Mankato, Minnesota.
052024
092024

Photo Credits: Getty Images, Science Source, Shutterstock
Production Contributors: Kenny Abdo, Jennie Forsberg, Grace Hansen, John Hansen
Design Contributors: Neil Klinepier

Library of Congress Control Number: 2023948511

Publisher's Cataloging in Publication Data

Names: Murray, Julie, author.
Title: Diplodocus / by Julie Murray
Description: Minneapolis, Minnesota : Abdo Zoom, 2025 | Series: Dinosaurs | Includes online resources and index.
Identifiers: ISBN 9781098285449 (lib. bdg.) | ISBN 9781098286149 (ebook) | ISBN 9781098286491 (Read-to-me eBook)
Subjects: LCSH: Dinosaurs--Juvenile literature. | Diplodocus--Juvenile literature. | Prehistoric animals--Juvenile literature. | Paleontology--Juvenile literature. | Extinct animals--Juvenile literature.
Classification: DDC 567.9--dc23

Table of Contents

Diplodocus 4

More Facts 22

Glossary 23

Index 24

Online Resources 24

Diplodocus

Diplodocus was a **sauropod** dinosaur. It lived 150 million years ago.

It lived near forests and water in what is North America today.

Diplodocus was a large dinosaur! It walked on four strong legs.

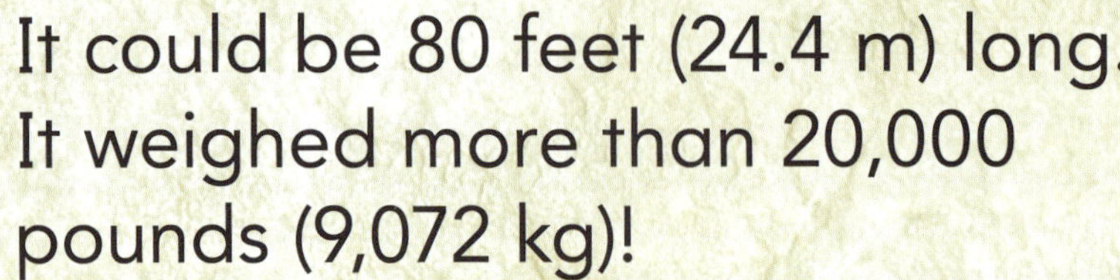

It could be 80 feet (24.4 m) long. It weighed more than 20,000 pounds (9,072 kg)!

Diplodocus had a long neck and tail. The neck and tail made up 80% of its length!

Diplodocus could use its tail like a whip. The tail also helped with balance.

The dinosaur had a small head. It had rake-like teeth for grabbing and pulling its food.

Diplodocus was a **herbivore**. It ate leaves high in trees and low on the ground.

The first Diplodocus **fossil** was discovered in 1877. The remains were found in Colorado.

More Facts

- *Diplodocus* means "double beam." This refers to the unique bones found on the underside of the dinosaur's tail.
- The dinosaur traveled in groups. Many of its **fossils** have been found together.
- It had flat teeth. It did not chew its food. It swallowed rocks to break up food in its stomach.

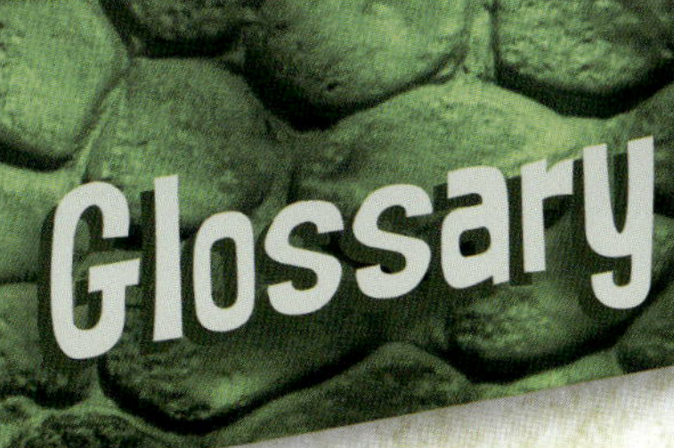

Glossary

fossil – the remains or trace of a living animal or plant from a long time ago. Fossils are found embedded in earth or rock.

herbivore – an animal that only feeds on plants.

sauropod – any of the suborder Sauropoda, such as Apatosaurus, characterized by having a large body with a long neck and tail, small head, and four legs.

Index

Colorado 20

food 17, 19

fossils 20

habitat 6

head 17

legs 9

neck 12

North America 6, 20

size 9, 10

tail 12, 14

teeth 17

Online Resources

To learn more about Diplodocus, please visit **abdobooklinks.com** or scan this QR code. These links are routinely monitored and updated to provide the most current information available.